Managing Your
401(k)

By Marc Robinson

TOP DOWN

TIME LIFE® BOOKS

Alexandria, Virginia

State Street Global Advisors: educating people about money

For 200 years, we have been in the banking business helping people manage and invest their money. We are a global leader in the investment management industry, serving institutions and individuals worldwide.

Our goal in creating this series is to give you unbiased, useful information that will help you manage your money. No product advertisements. No sales pitches. Just straightforward, understandable information.

Our ultimate hope is that after reading these books you feel more informed, more in control of your money, and perhaps most importantly, more able to successfully plan and reach your financial goals.

Time-Life Books is a division of
TIME LIFE INC.

Time-Life Custom Publishing
Vice President and Publisher: Terry Newell
Director of Sales: Neil Levin
Director, New Business Development: Phyllis A. Gardner
Senior Art Director: Christopher M. Register
Managing Editor: Donia Ann Steele
Production Manager: Carolyn Bounds
Quality Assurance Manager: James D. King

© 1997 Top Down

**For State Street Global Advisors,
The Lab:**
Clark Kellogg
Lynn Morgan
Sally Nellson
Paul Schwartz

For Top Down:
Marc Robinson
Lisa Braverman

Design: Maddocks and Company
Photography: Hervé Grison

The information contained in this publication is general in nature and is not intended to provide advice, guidance, or expertise of any nature regarding financial or investment decisions. Neither Time-Life Books, State Street Bank and Trust Company, Marc Robinson, nor Top Down make any representations or warranties with respect to the professional experience or credentials of the authors or contributors, or to the merits of the information or materials contained herein. The reader should consult independent financial advisors, investment professionals, and their attorneys prior to making any decision or plan.

Robinson, Marc, 1955-
    Managing your 401 (k) / by Marc Robinson.
             p.   cm. - - (Time Life Books your money matters)
    ISBN 0-7835-4812-5
    1. 401(k) plans–Management. 2. Compensation Management–United States.
    I. Title II. Series.
HF5549.5.C67R63 1997
332.024'01 - - dc21   96-340388
                           CIP

Contents

The big picture

A recent trend in this country has been toward less dependence on the government and employers to provide for financial security in retirement, and more toward individuals to provide for themselves. The main reason? Too many people and not enough federal money to go around.

So, where will your retirement money come from?

Bank and brokerage accounts

Any money you set aside after living expenses will help pay for retirement. You have lots of choices, from stocks and bonds to annuities and other securities.

Your home

During retirement, some homeowners increase their spending money by refinancing or by taking a second mortgage, a reverse mortgage, or a home equity loan. A home can be a risky source of income, however: Failure to make the loan payments could result in foreclosure.

Social Security

If you receive a paycheck, you probably pay Social Security taxes on your wages. That money isn't put away for you; it's used to pay the benefits of today's retirees (who paid Social Security taxes from their paychecks). In other words, working people support retirees who once were working people supporting other retirees. The average monthly benefit check from Social Security is a little over $700.

Experts predict that without an overhaul, Social Security will be bankrupt by 2030. Why? The number of people retiring each year is outpacing the number of people joining the work force. In 1960, 15 working people paying Social Security taxes covered the cost of one retiree's benefits. In 1996, that number shrank to 3.5. This trend of fewer workers paying for more retirees is expected to continue.

Self-funded plans

With money becoming tighter and companies becoming less willing to be legally responsible for their employees' financial security, 401(k)s are usually the company retirement plan of choice. Although many companies still contribute some money to each employee's account, the employee has chief responsibility for the saving and investing decisions (which is why these plans are called "self-funded").

Other plans include IRAs, SEP-IRAs, and SIMPLE accounts. An IRA gives tax breaks to individuals who save for retirement. SEP-IRAs do the same for self-employed people. SIMPLE accounts are the newest retirement plan offering tax breaks. They're available to companies employing 100 or fewer people.

Work

Many people continue working after retirement age to supplement their income. Social Security places an earnings limit on its recipients, however, and reduces the benefits of those who exceed the limit. For example, depending on age, a person could lose $1 in benefits for every $3 he or she goes over the earnings limit.

ompany-funded plans

ne companies operate a pension or a fit sharing plan, and they may contrib- money for employees, manage the estments, and provide a certain amount etirement income. In both plans, the pany is responsible for paying some ll of the benefits—and for making rt investment decisions. More and re companies are finding that these is are too expensive and place too much onsibility on company shoulders for ployees' retirement security.

What is a 401(k)?

Many people think a 401(k) is an investment. It isn't. A 401(k) is a plan created specifically to help people save for retirement. Your account is inside the plan; and you make investments inside your account. Most 401(k)s are "self-directed" plans. In other words, they're structured so that you direct the investing (and have ultimate responsibility for results). Officially, a 401(k) is a kind of "Defined Contribution Plan": it's a plan for contributing retirement savings that

is defined on three levels:

By the government

Two federal agencies supervise a set of rules and guidelines that apply to all 401(k) plans nationwide.

The Internal Revenue Service. A 401(k) plan is a "tax-qualified" plan. This means both you and your company get certain tax breaks—but only if you each follow the IRS rules so that the plan qualifies for those tax breaks. For example, the IRS sets rules on the process of contributing, the maximum to contribute, how and when to take withdrawals, what actions are taxable, and what penalties you and your company could face for breaking the rules.

The Department of Labor (DOL). They protect your rights as a 401(k) plan participant, seeing that your employer and plan trustees follow through on all required duties. They make sure that plans meet at least minimum federal requirements. They also require employers to give you sufficient information—in language you can understand—to make intelligent decisions.

By the company

Your employer is the plan sponsor—the creator—of your plan. It's the job of your company's top executives and benefits department to select the specific features, including investment options, that create a 401(k) plan within federal rules and guidelines. Of course, no company-wide plan can be all things to all people. Decisions, therefore, are typically based on the principle of the greatest good for the greatest number of people.

There are at least three good reasons why companies offer 401(k)s

1. It's one of the most valuable benefits a company can offer, so having as good a plan as possible helps attract and keep good workers.

2. In traditional pension plans, the company contributes all the money for the employees. Fewer companies can afford this, so many have switched to or added a 401(k), which is less expensive to fund and operate.

3. It gives more employees a chance to save. In pension plans, you generally don't keep any of the money put away for you unless you stay with the company for a predetermined number of years.

By you

At the plan's core is an investment account that you control. Within limits set by the IRS, your account gets special tax protection for money you put into it. The government has created the 401(k) plan as an incentive for long-term savings. Your company has created the tools you may use—and the rules you must follow—in its specific 401(k) plan. You, however, are the ultimate definer of your plan. You decide whether or not to participate. You decide how much to contribute (up to a maximum); what investments to buy, hold, and sell; when to withdraw money (within plan limits); and so on. Ultimately, your decisions determine how much you will save for retirement.

Looking inside a 401(k)

When you enroll in a 401(k) plan, you're not just investing, you're using a product. That product has several components, and each is critical to the operation of the plan. If you understand the basics of these components, you'll have an easier time using the available benefits. There are five **interconnected parts** to every plan.

Investment management

Since 401(k) plans are about investing, every plan has to have an investment component. It's your company's job to:

- hire one or more professional money management firms to offer investment options;
- select a diversified set of investments from those offered, and make them available to you;
- conduct periodic reviews to maintain the quality of the investment options and the managers;
- perform these tasks with "prudence" (reasonable care and wisdom);
- see that the work is performed within the framework of a written investment policy statement (which must be made available to you).

Recordkeeping

There is a legal requirement to track the activity of your account: what goes in, from whom; what goes out, to whom; what investments you make, when, using how much of your savings; and so on. Keeping accurate and timely records is one of the most crucial aspects of any plan. Without that, you won't have the proper information to make the best possible investment decisions. That's why many employers hire a professional recordkeeping company. The recordkeeper sends you an account statement—usually quarterly—that shows your choice of investments, their value, your investing activity, and other important information.

Reduced employer liability. ERISA section 404(c) provides optional guidelines employers can follow that will give participants more responsibility for investment decisions and reduce the company's liability. It doesn't completely eliminate responsibility, however. In fact, it requires employers to take a greater role by offering a broad range of investment options, sufficient investment instructions, and clear disclosure of relevant information and plan alternatives.

Communications

How do participants like
you learn how to use the
plan? How do they stay
informed about changes
and other events? And,
since all participants are
responsible for directing
their own investments,
ow do they get the information needed
o make intelligent choices? Employers who
ect to comply with ERISA section 404(c)
an reduce their potential liability, but in
turn have a greater duty to help you
ducate yourself about setting goals and
vesting for the long term through your
lan. They also have a legal duty to keep
ou well informed about how the plan
orks and any changes in benefits.

Plan administration

his is the procedural component of the
lan. It involves monitoring the health of
he plan, assisting and tracking every
ctivity of each participant, and adjusting
rocedures to meet new federal
equirements (or simply to make the plan
un smoothly). Your employer and the plan
rovider file all required
eports, prepare tax forms,
rovide and process loan
nd other forms, and
egularly monitor the plan
o see that it's being
perated fairly and meeting
ederal tests. They may also
andle payroll calculations,

ffer a customer service program, loans and
ther withdrawals, transfers of money when
mployees leave the company, and more.

Trustee services

Your company has what's called a "fiduciary"
responsibility, which simply means that it's
required to act on your behalf to protect
your interests. The company, therefore,
can sometimes be held accountable if something goes wrong with
the plan. Therefore,
the company appoints
trustworthy people
("trustees")—an outside
firm or senior officers—
to see that, essentially,
all goes as planned.

Mainly, a trustee supervises the plan to see
that plan assets are used only for the benefit
of the participants.

The name "401(k)" comes from the section
of the IRS regulations that created the plan
(Section 401(k) of the Internal Revenue Code).

Creating the plan

The success of a 401(k) plan depends on you and other employees using the plan wisely. If not enough employees participate or if they don't contribute enough salary, the plan may suffer. It coul cost your employer more than it's worth and create unhappy employees. The plan could even fail regulatory tests, creating more costs and efforts and damaging your employer's credibility. Your employer, therefore, must analyze the product in the context of the needs of employees versus what the company can afford

to balance the competing considerations.

Who is eligible. Some employers want to give employees the right to join immediately, as a job incentive. Others want to incentify employees to stay a year before enjoying the benefit. The law generally says you must be allowed to join if you're at least 21 and have worked at least 1,000 hours at the company during the year.

How much can be saved. The amount you can contribute is based on IRS rules, especially those relating to fairness. To keep companies from making plans too generous for higher paid employees at the expense of lower paid employees, the IRS enforces a complicated formula for determining maximum and minimum contributions. This is the formula's effect: People who don't participate or who contribute very little end up reducing the maximum amount highly paid employees can contribute.

Changes. How often to let you change your contribution amount is a payroll issue. It varies from daily to once a year. Payroll processing can be expensive, so cost affects this decision.

How much to match. Your company can match some of your contributions with contributions of their own. Typically, employers contribute between 1% to 3% of your salary, as long as you've put away at least as much. Despite the expense, employers include a match to attract and retain good workers. (A company may offer little or no match if it's spending a lot on other benefits, such as a pension plan or an extensive health plan.)

What you can keep. Any money your employer contributes isn't automatically yours to keep. You own only the "vested" amount; and vesting occurs based on a schedule. Employers choose one of these vesting schedules:

- "All-or-nothing" means you keep everything once you work at the company for a certain number of years. If you leave earlier, though, you get nothing.

- "Graded" means you gradually keep more money each year you stay, up to seven years. After that, you keep everything.

As with eligibility, employers try to balance the value of vesting as an incentive for you to stay longer with the company versus rewarding you for current efforts.

You may bear some of the costs
Most of your investment choices come with investment management fees. Take, for example, mutual funds. You don't pay these fees directly out of your account. They're taken out of the fund's total assets before the assets are split among shareholders like you, leaving slightly less money to share. Investment management fees typically range from .15% to 2.0%.

What investments. Employers must make three decisions here: how many investment choices to give you, what kind, and how often to let you switch choices.

The number and type are driven mostly by the diversity of the employee population. There should be sufficient choices for any employee to match his/her investment goals. More isn't always better; too many can be overwhelming. (Employers who want to comply with section 404(c) are advised to offer at least three choices, with different degrees of risk and reward.)

Your ability to switch investments can be as flexible as daily or as limited as quarterly. Some employers fear that, given the chance to switch daily, people will trade in and out too often and hurt investment performance. Even so, daily switching is common, even though it costs the most.

How to withdraw money. The ability to take out money is important to employees, but again, employers have to balance how much freedom to give you versus how to keep you from depleting your account. There's also the cost. For example, loans may have both application and maintenance costs, which many employers pass along as a $10–$50 loan fee.

What level of customer service. There are always questions and issues to face. The better the customer service, the more comfortable employees will feel about participating. Your employer can offer a toll-free phone number with live representatives, an automated phone service, or both.

Cost, as usual, is the balancing factor. Employers generally pay $10–$50 a year per participant for administrative services. The more extensive the service, the higher the fee. In order to be able to offer better services, some employers share the cost with employees through an administrative fee.

11

Putting in money

The money that goes into your account can come from a variety of sources. These sources have to be tracked by your plan's recordkeeping system—and are usually shown on your statement—becaus they may be taxed differently when you take the money out.

Here is the flow:

1. You redirect salary

By electing to contribute money to your 401(k), you postpone receiving that amount of your salary and redirect it into your 401(k) instead. Some plans let you elect an amount only once a year; others let you adjust it up and down as you assess your finances during the year.

Your employer contributes the amount to your 401(k) account in installments over the course of the year. Since this amount never makes it into your paychecks, your take-home pay goes down. But, since you've elected to take this salary as savings instead of as spending money, the IRS rewards you by saying the amount won't be counted as current income—and that lowers your income tax. That's why you'll see "pretax contributions" on your paystubs and statements; it's money that's put into savings for you before you pay taxes on it.

2. You contribute more

Many—not all—plans also let you make "aftertax contributions" if you want to save more than the plan rules allow for pretax contributions. In other words, you can contribute this money to your account instead of taking it as spending money— but only after the IRS takes its share.

Here, too, the money may come out of your paychecks in installments instead of going to you. Your paystub will itemize the aftertax amounts.

A dollar saved
Every dollar you save doesn't actually cost you a dollar of take-home pay. (Remember, since you're lowering your total income in the eyes of the IRS, you're given the benefit of paying less income tax.) For example, look at the effect of saving $2,000:

If you're in...	You take home...
15% bracket	$1,700 less
28% bracket	$1,440 less
33% bracket	$1,340 less

n 1996, no one could contribute more than
$9,500 of their pretax income. (That amount may
go up slightly each year.)

n 1996, the total of all the year's contributions to
all plans couldn't be more than 25% of your salary,
or $30,000, whichever was less.

Plan limits
1. Typically, you're permitted to save at least 1% but no more than 15% of your pretax salary.

2. Employers may make matching contributions that total between 1% and 3% of your salary. (So, if you save 7% and the company adds 3%, you're saving 10% of your salary—while only contributing 7%.)

3. Your **employer** puts in **more**

Many employers choose to make "matching contributions," based on the amount you contribute from your salary. It's essentially free money—an instant profit. This can be an expensive proposition for a company, and is a powerful benefit found nowhere else in the world of investing.

The amount of a "match" varies widely. It could be 10¢ for every $1 you contribute or $3 for every $2 you contribute. Most companies are somewhere in between. (The company may match your contribution using company stock instead of cash.)

4. Your **account** accumulates

Your account now may hold at least three kinds of contributions. Many plans provide account statements that track them separately. Here's why:

Pretax money. When you take this money out (except by loan), it's subject to income taxation because you've ended the promise to save by removing the money from the tax shelter and turning it into spending money.

Aftertax money. This money isn't taxed when you withdraw it because you've already paid income taxes on it. Whatever amount this money earns while in the account, however, is taxable when it comes out.

Employer match. This money may not be yours to keep until you have been with your company for a certain number of years. There are also separate tax issues.

13

Taxes: pro and con

To encourage long-term savings, the government offers people tax breaks. To discourage people from changing their minds—or from using their hard-earned savings frivolously—they've installed serious tax restrictions.

Here's the good and bad news:

Tax savings

These are the tax breaks offered to induce you to save.

Income tax deferral. The money you contribute to a 401(k) plan account is subtracted from your annual income and isn't taxed. As far as the IRS is concerned, it's as if you didn't earn it—in that year. If you take it out, however, you will pay taxes on it. A 401(k) plan, therefore, is called a "tax-deferred" plan (not a tax-free plan) because you defer (postpone) paying income tax on the money you contribute until you remove it from its tax-protected haven.

Here's the effect:

Say you make $30,000 and elect to save $2,400. You'll pay income taxes as if you only earned $27,600. In the 28% tax bracket, that will put $672 in your pocket that would have gone to the IRS. So, instead of putting $2,400 into savings and taking home $2,400 less, you'll only take home $1,728 less ($2,400 - $672).

Tax-deferred growth. The other big benefit is tax deferral on earnings. Any money earned by investments you make in your 401(k) account goes untaxed until withdrawn permanently (the taxes are deferred—delayed until a later date). If you're in a lower tax bracket when you retire, that could save you money.

Rollovers. You can take your money out of a 401(k) plan and still keep the tax benefit if you "roll over" the money into another tax-qualified plan (generally, either another company retirement plan or an IRA). Within that rule is another rule: If you put the money into a "Rollover IRA" you open specifically for that purpose, you'll be allowed to roll it over again into another 401(k) plan or other plan at a later date (if your new company's plan rules permit it). You can also make "partial rollovers," but any amount rolled over becomes taxable.

Forward averaging. If you take out the entire amount in one lump sum and you're $59\frac{1}{2}$ or older, you can take advantage of a one-time special rule that could lower your taxes. It's called "five-year averaging" or "forward averaging," and it works like this: You take the money all at once, but are allowed to pay taxes as if you took it in installments over five years. Check with your tax advisor to see if you can use it and what effect it will have on your taxes.

Triple tax trap. If you don't replace the 20% withholding amount with your own money and deposit it into another retirement plan, you will face several negative consequences. You won't get back the withholding, it will become income to you so you will pay income tax on it, plus you will pay a 10% penalty on it for early withdrawal (if you're younger than 59 ½).

don't pay income taxes or an early withdrawal
halty on loans since you will be putting the money
ck into your account. If, however, you don't pay it
ck on time (usually within 5 years), or make at least
arterly payments, the IRS considers it a withdrawal.
hat case, you will pay income taxes and the 10%
ly withdrawal penalty.

Divorces
A divorced spouse who has received a Qualified
Domestic Retirement Order (QDRO) is allowed to
withdraw his/her portion of the money without paying
the 10% penalty.

ax **payments**

ou can expect to pay one or more of the
lowing taxes when you take money out
the plan.

come taxes. Since 401(k) money grows "tax
ferred," not "tax free," any money you
rmanently withdraw must be reported on
ur tax return as income. Be aware that
e money you withdraw is added to any
her income you earn during the year, so
may be enough to push you into a
gher tax bracket.

addition, any money earned by "after-
x contributions" is taxable once it's
moved permanently from the account.

rly withdrawal penalty. Since the IRS gives
ou a tax break for saving money in a
01(k) plan, you're penalized if you change
ur mind. In addition to income taxes,
ou pay a 10% penalty on money with-
awn before you're 59½. The exceptions:
you take a loan, become disabled (under
e plan's definition), die, or leave your job
ter you turn age 55.

tomatic withholding. Your company may
required to withhold 20% of your
ithdrawal and send it to the IRS as a
repayment on your income taxes. If, at
x time, you owe more, you'll have to
ay the additional taxes out of your own
ocket. If you owe less, the IRS will send
ou a refund. There's one exception:
here's no withholding if you have your
mployer transfer money directly to another
ualified retirement plan.

Minimum required distribution penalty. If you are
retired and at least 70½, you must make
minimum annual withdrawals (the first one
must be by April 1 of the year after you
turn 70½). These withdrawals are based on
your life expectancy or the joint life
expectancy of you and your spouse. If you
withdraw less than the IRS minimum, you
pay a 50% penalty on the amount you
fall short. For example, if the required
minimum is $3,000 and you only withdraw
$1,000, you'll pay a $1,000 penalty
(50% of the $2,000 shortfall).

Estate taxes. When you die, your 401(k)
money may be subject to estate taxes at a
rate from 37% to 55%. There are ways to
avoid—or at least delay—this payment.
First, any 401(k) money left to a spouse
avoids estate tax (although there may be
estate taxes on it when your spouse dies).
Second, up to $600,000
of your assets, including
401(k) money, can
go to anyone estate
tax free. The rules
are complicated, so
talk to a tax advisor.

The effect of postponed taxes

Besides allowing you to report less taxable income, the government also lets you postpone (or defer) paying taxes on any money earned in your 401(k) plan account until you permanently withdraw it. This "tax-deferred" growth means you'll have more money working

to earn more money.

Compound growth

The chart on these pages is only a hypothetical example, but it illustrates how one of life's truisms—it takes money to make money—is even truer when money grows without being taxed in a 401(k) plan.

This example assumes $1,200 contributed every year and compares tax-deferred savings with savings in a taxable account. Both the taxable account and the tax-deferred 401(k) account earn 8% a year over the course of 30 years.

The earnings in the 401(k) account aren't taxed. Every dollar is reinvested and continues to earn more money. In this example, however, the earnings in the taxable account are taxed at 28% a year.

What's the impact of that tax bite? Every year, the 401(k) plan account keeps all its earnings while the taxable account earns 28% less than the 401(k)—and gradually falls farther and farther behind.

Year 10

Year 0

**Tax-deferred savings
$158,890**

**Taxable savings
$102,634**

Year 30

Year 20

sumptions: $1,200 to start, $1,200 per year, taxable versus tax-deferred savings at 8% over 30 years, 28% tax bracket.

te of caution: This chart is for illustrative purposes only and isn't intended to reflect the performance
an actual investment. Investments typically do not grow at an even rate and may experience losses.

Tapping the account

The rules governing 401(k) plans form a system of incentives and deterrents designed to help you keep saving until retirement. Nevertheless, there may be times when you need the money sooner, so the rules also include some exceptions. There are limits to these exceptions set by law, although companies can choose to set even tighter limits if they're concerned about employees plundering their retirement savings.

You have two choices:

Borrow and repay it

Many plans let you borrow from your account. Most limit you to one loan at a time. Some plans let you borrow for any reason, while others require you to prove the loan is for an "emergency" (defined by the people in your company who created the plan).

How much? A plan can be more restrictive, but by law, you can borrow the lesser of $50,000 or 50% of money you own completely ("vested" money)—minus the highest outstanding balance you had on a 401(k) loan in the previous year.

There are often two ways to request a loan—by phone or by form. Either way, there's no lengthy credit check because it's already your money.

Not deductible. Loan payments aren't tax deductible: You're returning money you already contributed and on which you already got a tax break, so the IRS won't let you deduct it a second time.

Loans by phone. Not all plans allow loans by phone, but if yours does, the check (or the forms) will arrive within days of your request. Often, by simply signing the back of the check you agree to the terms of the loan, including the interest rate, repayment schedule, and automatic repayments from future paychecks. (The terms will come in writing either with or before the check.)

Loans by form. You get the form (which is the loan agreement) from the benefits office and send it to the plan provider. It may then be sent to your employer for approval and sent back to the provider. That could take a week or more.

Payback time. By law, a loan must be fully repaid within 5 years unless you use the money to buy your main home. In that case you might have 20–30 years to repay. Payments are in regular, equal installments. Your paystubs will show each loan payment amount.

You're repaying yourself—with interest. The interest rate is usually the prime rate (listed in most newspapers) plus one or two percent. It's typically lower than credit card and bank loan rates.

ɔu make a "financial hardship" withdrawal, you will
e to take more than the hardship amount: You may
charged a 10% "early withdrawal" penalty and have
% withheld for taxes. So, for example, if you need
000, the IRS will let you withdraw $2,600 to cover
withholding and penalty.

won't pay the 10% penalty if you're:
aying medical bills above 7.5% of your income;
sabled (by your plan's definition);
ver age 55; or
e divorcing spouse of the employee
vho has a QDRO).

Special loan rules

As long as you repay loans on schedule, there are
no penalties or taxes. But if you leave the company,
you may have to repay the loan in full immediately. If
you can't, the amount will be reported to the IRS
as a withdrawal. That will trigger the 10% penalty.

ake and keep it

e IRS lets people withdraw money for
e of four "financial hardship" reasons; to

buy a primary residence;

pay for college;

pay major, unreimbursed medical
expenses; or

avoid foreclosure or eviction.

ɪns are allowed to have more lenient
ɪits. Check with your benefits office. In
y case, you must show proof of how
ɪu'll use the money and that you're not
rrowing more than you need. The proof
ght be the sales contract on your new
me or copies of medical or tuition bills.

Since you have to prove need, the process
of hardship withdrawals takes longer. In
most cases, you'll start by filling out a form
from your benefits office and sending it to
the plan provider, who will send it to your
employer for approval. Even if you can
make a request by phone, expect the
process to take several weeks.

Leaving the plan

Eventually, you'll leave your company, either for a new job or for retirement. Federal regulations, taxes, and penalties will shape how and when you can take your savings with you. Your plan may also have restrictions. At that point, you will deal

with the money in **one of these ways:**

Take it as **cash**

You can take all your money in cash. Your company will withhold 20% and send it to the IRS as a prepayment on your income taxes (to protect the IRS from your spending it all and having nothing left to pay). You'll get a check for the rest.

At tax time, you may also have to pay a 10% "early withdrawal" penalty. You avoid the penalty if you:

- are age 59½ or older;
- leave your company and are over age 55;
- become disabled, as defined by your company's plan (most plans consider you disabled if you can't work enough to support yourself at any time in the near future); or
- die, which means the money goes to your primary beneficiary (automatically your spouse unless you name someone else).

Portability. Many plans accept money from other 401(k)s to make retirement benefits m "portable." That way people who change jobs don't lose the tax benefits on the money they've saved for retirement.

quired withdrawals

nerally, the IRS makes you take a minimum amount
ch year once you're age 70 ½ and are retired.
tually, you have until April 1 following the year you
n 70 ½.) The amount is based on the life
ectancy of a person your age and is equal to your
count balance divided by the number of years you

are expected to live. (If you're 70 ½, the IRS says your
life expectancy is 16 years.)
To reduce your required withdrawals, you may be able
to use the combined life expectancy for you and your
spouse, rather than your life expectancy alone. Talk to
a tax advisor for assistance.

Transfer it

o continue receiving the tax benefits,
ou can transfer the money to another
tirement plan—either your next employer's
an (if that's allowed) or an IRA (which
ou'll open specifically for this purpose).
here are two ways to make the transfer:

ompany direct. You can fill out a form and
sk your company to transfer the money
irectly into another tax-qualified plan.
ince the money never really leaves the
helter of a retirement plan, you avoid the
o% withholding and the 10% early
ithdrawal penalty.

n your own. Even if you take it as cash
and the company withholds 20%), you still
ave 60 days in which to transfer some or
ll of the money into an IRA (the 80%
ou received, plus the other 20%, which
ust come from your own pocket).
Vhatever isn't transferred into your
RA may be subject to income tax and
e 10% penalty.

Leave it

Some companies let employees leave their
money in the plan, even if they go to
work for someone else. This may be a
good choice if, after comparing the new
employer's plan, you like the current plan's
investments and customer service. By
federal regulation, if you have at least
$3,500 in your account, your company is
required to give you this option.

> **Rollover.** Transferring 401(k) money to an
> IRA is called "rolling it over." Unless you
> keep this rollover separate from other IRA
> accounts by opening a separate Rollover
> IRA, a new employer won't accept it into
> their 401(k). In other words, the money
> must remain "pure" 401(k) money to
> continue benefiting from 401(k) rules.

Your employer's investment options

In setting up a plan, employers are given all kinds of investment options. It's your employer's job to sift through the choices and offer a plan that allows people with any strategy—conservative, moderate, or aggressive—to select proper investments to meet that strategy. The specific investment choices typically

come from these broad categories:

Mutual funds

Many companies selling 401(k) plans offer employers a selection of mutual funds. These are "retail" products: The same funds are sold directly to individuals and appear in the newspaper every day.

A plan may be charged the same fees as individual investors. For example, there's often a "12b-1" fee charged to cover sales and marketing expenses (which can be a large portion of the overall fee because of the efforts needed to sell directly to the public).

There are probably at least 20 different kinds of funds to choose from. Some are aggressive, others moderate, and others conservative. Within these categories, a fund could focus on U.S. stocks or international stocks; on stocks of large companies or small companies; on U.S. or international bonds; on long-term bonds or short-term bonds; on mixtures of stocks and bonds; on mixtures of U.S. and international securities—the list goes on.

Commingled (pooled) funds

Sometimes an investment management firm offers to create a mix of investments specifically for a corporate client. These pooled funds are managed similarly to mutual funds, but aren't sold in the retail market to individuals. They may also have lower expenses than mutual funds: There are no sales and marketing expenses (since they're not sold to the public), and investment management fees may also be lower. These savings are passed on to you.

he investment selection must appeal to a broad nge of people, so demographics count; for ample, the range in income levels, educational vels, and investment experience. Age also matters a t. Young employees with many years until retirement ay want investments with long-term growth potential. mployees near retirement will need choices with ore short-term safety.

Then there are the costs. Some types of funds cost more to run than others. International funds are among the most expensive since they deal with complexities like foreign currencies, overseas trading, and more difficult research. Index funds are among the least expensive because they aren't actively managed. Since you'll share these costs, employers factor cost into their selection.

ifestyle/Asset allocation funds

hese are pooled funds or mutual funds hat have been premixed to suit the needs nd goals of people according to their ifferent stages of life and attitudes toward westing. You don't have to try to create our own mix of investments. Instead, you mply select a fund that's designed for a erson in your stage of life or with similar oals. Many employers select funds that can erve all employees: conservative, moderate, nd aggressive.

ICs

A GIC is a Guaranteed Investment Contract, offered to retirement plans. Essentially, this is a product offered by an nsurance company or other financial nstitution that pays interest regularly to our company 401(k) over a certain eriod of time.

The promise to make regular interest ayments and repay the principal is only s good as the creditworthiness of the ompanies making the payments. You can heck a GIC's credit rating in materials usually found with your enrollment kit.

Company stock

Some companies offer their own stock as an investment option. This is a good way to participate in the success of your company, but it's a different kind of investment than professionally managed funds. Since your money is in one stock rather than a collection of investments, there's more risk than in spreading around your investments: The growth of your money depends entirely on how well the company does. If it does well and the stock price goes up, your investment will grow. If the company runs into difficulties and the stock price falls, your investment will lose value.

23

Your investment choices

Creating your personal mix is called "asset allocation" (a term you may often see, since it's commonly used by the financial industry). It means allocating your assets as you see fit according to your personal situation. Once your employer has selected the investments to offer all the participants, it's your turn

to **make the selections** that look best for you.

Protection

Most likely, you'll be offered one of the following, but not both. They serve the same function: investing for short periods at low risk.

Money market funds. When you invest in this type of mutual fund, you're making short-term (sometimes literally overnight) loans and receiving interest on those loans. The interest rates are low but so is the risk of losing money (although the risk of not earning enough to reach your goal may be high). Money market funds are often considered "parking places." Investors tend to feel safe parking their money there before taking it out to spend it, or while deciding on their next strategic move.

GICs. A GIC is often called a "stable value investment." In other words, you get back what you invested plus predetermined interest. GICs often pay higher interest than money market funds (but neither typically pays as much as bond funds).

Moderate growth

You may also be given a choice to earn relatively predictable amounts at a somewhat faster pace.

Fixed income (bond) funds. By investing in these funds, you lend money either to corporations or to governmental bodies. In return, you're paid interest (that's the "fixed income"). These loans are for longer periods than the short terms of money market funds, and the risks of losing money are generally higher. That risk (your likelihood of being repaid in full) is mainly determined by the creditworthiness of the borrowers (their projected ability to repay) and the length of the loan (the longer the time, the more chance of something negative happening). It's a myth that your investment is totally safe in fixed income funds. The value of your shares can rise and fall—in some cases, with as much unpredictability as stock funds.

Faster growth

You may be given a choice to try to earn money at an even faster pace.

Balanced funds and growth & income funds. These funds do a bit of strategy-mixing for you by balancing investments in both stocks and bonds. The goal is to earn some predictable income (through interest and dividends) and also go for higher returns (through rises in stock prices). "Balance" also applies to the approach to risk and reward: The fund managers continually try to balance the risks they're willing to take against the aggressiveness with which they're willing to seek the best returns.

Even faster growth

Growth funds. These funds look for stocks that appear to have a lot of room for their prices to grow. Growth funds could buy small, medium, or large company stocks. Generally, the more small companies there are in the fund, the more aggressively the managers are pursuing growth.

International and emerging market funds. Since over half the world's investment opportunities are overseas, many plans offer international funds. Often, when our stock market is down, some foreign markets are doing well. These funds, therefore, let you "diversify" (spread) your money among more opportunities. Investing in foreign markets tends to be riskier than most domestic investing, since it involves different currencies and unfamiliar economies and politics.

Investment strategies

There's no single right way to invest. What you do with the money depends on what you want it to do for you. For example, if you have a short time to make a lot of money, you'll need an aggressive strategy—or a willingness to settle for falling short of your goal. If you have a lot of time to make a little amount of money, you can invest cautiously—earning smaller amounts in more predictable investments—and still reach your goal. In all cases, though, there are

four questions to help you take aim:

When will you need it?

Some time frames are fairly predictable, such as when you'll reach retirement, when the kids will go to college, or maybe, when you'll buy a house. Of course, there are also plenty of unpredictable events that could cause you to tap into your savings ahead of schedule.

Time is a crucial component of strategy. In general, the more time you have, the less you need to worry about up-and-down swings in price. If you have five years or less, your goals are considered short term. If you have 10 years or more, your goals are considered long term.

Where are you now?

What is your current life status and the state of your finances? Your 401(k) plan decisions should fit into your overall pictur How much money do you make and how much can you save? Are you married or single; with or without children?

The number of people you're saving for will influence your choices. So will the number of people saving. If two family members are saving in retirement plans, consider the overall savings and how to coordinate the two so you're not duplicating efforts.

How much will you need?

By looking at what you have now and the total amount you'll eventually need, you'll know how much more to try to accumulate.

What are the risks?

The first risk of investing is "market risk," the chance of losing money if the value of your investment drops. Market risk is due, essentially, to the unpredictability of the economy and the psychology of buyers and sellers. That might seem to dictate putting money in investments known to hold their price while earning only small amounts. An investment still loses money, though, if it doesn't earn enough to outpace inflation. That's because, if you earn $2 to buy a product and inflation makes the product cost $3, you've actually lost $1.

The other important risk is "shortfall risk," the possibility of falling short of your goal. If your investment doesn't grow enough, you might not have enough money to live on during retirement. Shortfall risk occurs when people choose investments that mostly preserve, rather than grow, their money. Many people think retirement savings belong in the safest investments, and they avoid market risk—the short-term ups and downs. But what's worse, unpredictable price fluctuations or the possibility of not having enough money to meet expenses?

Matching choices to goals

Picking investments is an ongoing process. As years pass, goals usually change. Shifting strategy to match your time frame and goals, therefore, is an important part of investing. At first, you may want your money to grow as much as possible—particularly if retirement is many years away. But as you get closer to needing the cash, you may want to earn less interest in order to give more protection to what you've got. Consider how long you have to invest and how you want to split your money between different growth and protection strategies. This chart shows various kinds of investments that have historically achieved different performance levels

within the time you have.

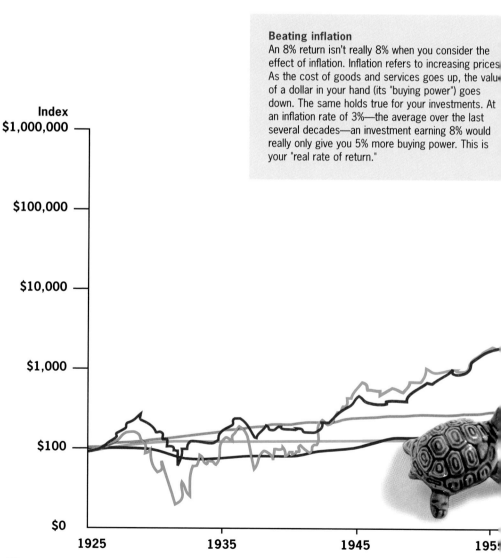

Beating inflation
An 8% return isn't really 8% when you consider the effect of inflation. Inflation refers to increasing prices. As the cost of goods and services goes up, the value of a dollar in your hand (its "buying power") goes down. The same holds true for your investments. At an inflation rate of 3%—the average over the last several decades—an investment earning 8% would really only give you 5% more buying power. This is your "real rate of return."

Index
$1,000,000

$100,000

$10,000

$1,000

$100

$0

1925   1935   1945   1955

Time, return and risk

How long do you have to reach your goals? How much will you need your money to grow over that time period? Which types of investments in the chart below have historically reached your goal within your time frame? They're not necessarily the ones with the highest returns.

Consider the frequency of price rises and drops (the "volatility") that have historically occurred during your time frame. For example, though small company stocks had the best returns over many time frames, they also had many of the sharpest ups and downs. The risk of volatility is in its unpredictability: If you'll need money on short notice and may have to sell during a dip, the risk of bad timing may not be worth the potential reward. That's why, when many investors get closer to needing their money, they shift into investments with more price stability.

If you can leave your money alone for a long time (the way you're supposed to in a 401(k) plan account), the amount of short-term ups and downs may not be bothersome as long as there's a general upward trend.

A word of caution: You can only use charts like this as guides. The types of investments shown here aren't all-inclusive; they're only indicative of the variety. Most important, there's no guarantee that what happened in the past will reoccur in the future.

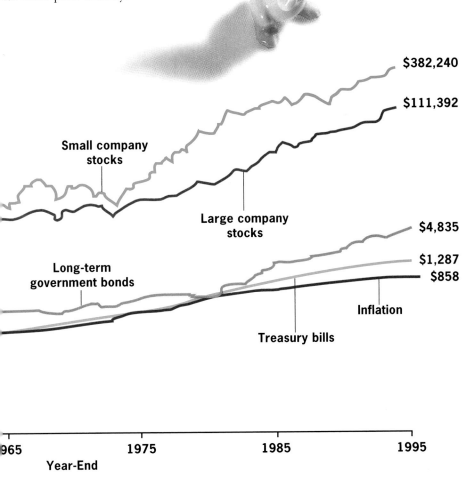

Small company stocks

$382,240

$111,392

Large company stocks

Long-term government bonds

$4,835

$1,287

$858

Inflation

Treasury bills

1965   1975   1985   1995

Year-End

Communication

Though you're responsible for your investments, it's in your employer's best interest to give you sufficient access to helpful information so that you may make informed decisions. Some things employers are required to tell you; the rest is what they think you should know. Here is a rundown of typical plan communications,

focusing on what you might like to know.

Basic investment information

To help you understand what you could invest in, and the potential risks and rewards, plans typically provide these tools:

Prospectus. This legal document is given to you either before you invest in a mutual fund or at the time you invest. Included are financial highlights and fees and other charges, rules governing the fund, profiles of the investment managers, and more. Most plans provide it to participants. (You can always request one by phone.) Pooled funds don't have prospectuses, so you should look for information on fact sheets supplied by your employer.

Fact sheets. These explain what each investment is and how it works. They typically consist of one or two pages of an overview of such topics as the specific kinds of securities bought and sold, historical performance (sometimes compared with an industry benchmark), potential risks, and more.

Toll-free phone number. Plans with 800 numbers usually provide automated performance information on each investment option. Some plans also have customer service representatives who will answer questions and help you conduct transactions.

Magazines, newsletters. Many plans provide at least a semiannual newsletter or a magazine. Topics range from specific ideas to in-depth investment and personal finance explanations.

Your account status

This information may come from two sources.

Account statement. This tells you where your money is invested, how much you've earned or lost, how much you and your employer have contributed, the status of any loans or other withdrawals, and details of any activity since the last statement was prepared. You must receive at least one a year, although most plans send statements quarterly.

Toll-free phone number. This lets you get automated, instant, current account information as well as information on investment choices, loans, and other plan features. These phone services may also let you make transfers, change elections, and direct many other activities for your account.

Changes in the plan

You're kept informed of administrative changes in a number of ways, depending on urgency and importance. There are legally required notices. You can also look for changes in rules, investment options, and plan features in your newsletter, statement stuffers, and brochures. (If money was spent to create a glossy brochure, expect the changes to be important.)

In-depth investment assistance

Many plan providers give employers interactive products to distribute to employees. These tools allow people to customize answers to their own needs and even form an actual working plan, rather than simply consider what they might do.

Software. People with access to computers may receive software that uses interactive exercises to guide them through a self-analysis and educational program.

Worksheets and questionnaires. The low-tech version of software, these worksheets can still reward users with useful end results.

The plan in detail

Upon enrollment, employers give you a booklet called the Summary Plan Description (SPD)—although it may have a friendlier title. This is the reference document for the plan. Although it's relatively long, it's objective and is usually written in simplified language. Among other things, it explains how to take action if you feel your rights have been violated. You should receive an updated SPD once every five years—sooner if there's been a major change in the plan.

The SPD is actually a summary of the Plan Document, which contains the full legal guidelines. You may request a copy from your employer.

On-line access. In the last few years, "high tech" meant giving you current account information through a toll-free phone line. Today, many plans give you access to Web sites.

31

The length of participation

Participating in your 401(k) plan isn't a one-time event. Once a company rolls out a plan, it takes on a whole life cycle that evolves as time passes and that affects the plan's value to you. The government may change 401(k) plan regulations, your company may change plan features, and your needs and goals will probably change.

Here is how it rolls out:

Become eligible. You're at least 21 years old and have worked at least 1,000 hours at your company during the year. These are IRS guidelines. Your company's rules can be more lenient, but not more restrictive.

Join the plan. On the entry date set by your company, you enroll, decide how much to contribute, and choose who gets the money if you die (your beneficiary). If you are married and the beneficiary isn't your spouse, you must get the spouse's written permission.

Select investments. You choose your initial investments. You can elect to split your contributions among several choices based on your investment goals.

Contribute. The money comes out of each paycheck in installments over the year.

Receive extra savings. Your company may make matching contributions to your account.

Get vested. Over time (no more than seven years), you earn the right to keep the money your employer contributes. Money you contribute is immediately 100% "vested"—it's always yours to keep.

Make changes. You can fine-tune your decisions as you go. Some plans allow changes at any time. Others place limitations, such as once a quarter or once a year.

Reevaluate goals. Life situations change. Goals change. Local and national economies change. At times, you'll look at your entire strategy to see if every part still makes sense. (Experts recommend reassessing goals once a year; more often if there's an unexpected change.)

p the account. You may be able to borrow oney or make hardship withdrawals to over certain major expenses before you ach age 59½.

ave the company. The vested portion of our 401(k) account is portable. Take all some in cash and pay taxes on it, plus 10% early withdrawal penalty if you're nder age 55. You can delay taxes by ansferring some or all of it to a new nployer's qualified retirement plan (if ey accept it) or an IRA. You may also able to leave it in the company plan, here it can continue to grow tax deferred.

rn age 59 ½. From here on, there are no ore early withdrawal penalties. You may ithdraw money and roll it into another ualified plan (e.g., IRA) within 60 days to oid paying income taxes.

Retire. You decide how to take payments. You can set up a schedule to get regular payments. Or, like most people, take it out as you need it. You pay income taxes on whatever you take out. If you take it all in one lump sum, you could receive favorable tax treatment.

Turn age 70 ½ and are retired. Each year from this point on, you withdraw at least the minimum required by the IRS. Annual installments are based on a formula that is based on the number of years you're expected to live.

Death. Whatever is in your account goes to the person you named as beneficiary. This person can take the money in cash and pay taxes, or delay taxes by leaving the money in the plan for a certain number of years (based on how old you were when you died). If you have no surviving spouse and didn't name a beneficiary, your plan's rules will govern where the money will go.

Who's who

Plan providers

These are the financial companies who sell the services your employer buys to create a 401(k) plan. Most are investment management firms, mutual fund companies, banks, insurance companies, recordkeeping companies, or benefits consulting firms.

Brokerage firms

Some plans offer an option that lets employees invest in individual stocks and bonds in addition to mutual funds. In that case, the employee opens an account at a brokerage firm and a broker does the buying and selling. The broker makes a fee (called a "commission") on every trade. A full-service broker will give you advice on investment decisions. A discount broker will only handle the trades, leaving all decisions up to the employee.

Customer service representatives

These people are hired by the plan provider to answer your questions, resolve problems, or simply take orders for transactions. They're usually available through a toll-free number. Many of them are well versed in your investment options and can help you conduct transactions.

Employee benefits/human resources

As employees of your firm, they help run the plan from the company's side. They help you join and set up your contributions through payroll. They also work with the plan provider to create the materials that will teach you about your plan and how to use it. They may be the source for beginning a loan or withdrawal, and for any plan documents you want to review.

Plan trustees

These people generally are responsible for supervising the plan's money. They make sure, for example, it's invested properly. They also supervise the plan's operations, making sure all the governmental rules and regulations are followed. They could be company officers, a bank, or another financial institution.

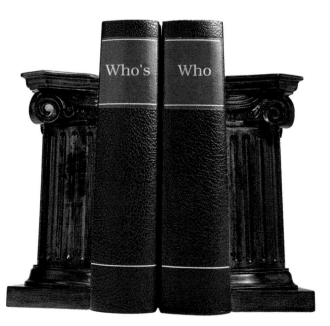

[Appendix]

If you contribute to your company retirement plan, you can also contribute to an IRA. There are, however, restrictions.

The amount you will be allowed to deduct for your IRA contributions will vary depending on your adjusted gross income (income minus all allowable deductions).

This is how it works:

For single people:

If your adjusted gross income is:

$25,000 or less	the IRA contribution is fully deductible
$25,001 - $35,000	the IRA contribution is partially deductible
	(talk to a tax advisor to determine the deductible amoun
$35,001 or more	the IRA contribution is not deductible

For married people:

If your combined adjusted gross income is:

$40,000 or less	the IRA contribution is fully deductible
$40,001 - $50,000	the IRA contribution is partially deductible
	(talk to a tax advisor to determine the deductible amoun
$50,001 or more	the IRA contribution is not deductible

hen you withdraw money, there are two effects:

- Since the money you take comes out of your account, you'll have less money in the account.
- There will be less money working to earn more money. Over time, your account will grow more slowly than it would have without the loan or hardship withdrawal—especially since every dollar in the account grows tax deferred.

he following is a hypothetical example comparing how much it could cost in the long run to take a an or a hardship withdrawal vs. leaving your savings alone. This is only one example. Don't use it r any purpose other than to understand the concept: how you lose earning power when you remove oney from the account.

he example:
ou're 35. You have $40,000 in savings. You're in the 28% tax bracket. You want to take ut $15,000. (If the withdrawal is a loan, you'll pay it back in installments over five years.) ere's how each decision will affect your savings.

	To borrow $15,000	To withdraw $15,000*	To leave savings
mount in savings	$40,000	$40,000	$40,000
arly withdrawal penalty aid (if under age 59½)	$0	$2,419	$0
8% tax on withdrawal	$0	$6,774	$0
otal amount withdrawn	$15,000	$24,193	$0
emaining balance	$25,000	$15,807	$40,000
lonthly payments**	$304	$304	$304
otal savings after 10 years	$88,786	$71,611	$125,312
otal savings at 65	$437,430	$352,815	$573,601
otal after taxes	$314,949	$304,415	$412,993
otal cost of choice***	$98,044	$108,578	$0

ou'll need to withdraw extra money to cover the cost of taxes and penalties. If you qualify for a hardship withdrawal, the IRS allows ou to withdraw enough money from your 401(k) account to cover any taxes and penalties you owe on the amount you need. Check ith your benefits department for the specifics of your plan.

*This example assumes an 8% interest rate on your loan. In the withdrawal example, it assumes you will save the equivalent of the onthly loan payments in a taxable account earning 8% compounded monthly (with earnings taxed annually at 28%). In the savings xample, it assumes that the monthly contributions to the 401(k) account continue. After the loan, contributions continue to the 401(k).

**The total savings amount in the withdrawal example includes both 401(k) and taxable savings.

When a company makes matching contributions to your 401(k), you may be required to stay with th
company a certain period of time before you'll be permitted to reap the benefits of its generosity. **
are two representative schedules.

Typical "graded" vesting schedule

Years employed at the company	Employer contributions you may keep (vested amount)
Less than one year	0%
One year but less than two	20%
Two years but less than three	40%
Three years but less than four	60%
Four years but less than five	80%
Five years or longer	100%

Maximum allowable vesting schedule

Years employed at the company	Employer contributions you may keep (vested amount)
Less than three years	0%
Three years but less than four	20%
Four years but less than five	40%
Five years but less than six	60%
Six years but less than seven	80%
Seven years or longer	100%

his table illustrates the difference in the amount of spending money you'll have after saving in a
01(k) account and saving on your own. Not only do you end up with more money by saving in the
01(k), you also don't have to worry about the discipline of putting away money every month,
ecause the contributions occur automatically.

	Saving $1,800 before taxes	Saving $1,800 after taxes
Annual income	$25,000	$25,000
Pretax savings	1,800	0
Taxable income	$23,200	$25,000
Taxes at 28%	6,500	7,000
Net take-home pay	$16,700	$18,000
Aftertax savings	0	1,800
Total spending money	$16,700	$16,200

The following is a table showing how many years people are expected to live after retirement. These figures are used by the IRS in calculating certain requirements; for example, the minimum amounts you must receive from your account each year after age 70 ½.

Of course, these figures are only averages. Many people live longer than the expected number of years. In fact, some experts recommend that, to be conservative, you should add approximately seven years to the life expectancy listed below when you calculate the amount of money you will need during your years in retirement.

Retirement age	An individual should live...	One of the two in a couple should live...
55	another 29 years	another 34 years
60	another 24 years	another 30 years
65	another 20 years	another 24 years
70	another 16 years	another 21 years

Social Security benefits

This table gives an indication of how much you could expect to receive in Social Security benefits annually, assuming there are no changes in Social Security laws. This chart uses 1996 figures.

Your current age	\$20K	\$30K	\$40K	\$50K	\$60K
25	\$9,432	\$12,836	\$14,412	\$15,912	\$17,820
35	9,432	12,836	14,412	15,912	17,784
45	9,432	12,836	14,412	15,912	17,784
55	9,432	12,836	14,304	15,444	16,428
65	9,420	12,584	13,812	14,932	14,976

Your current income (spanning the income columns)